Nelson Grammar International
Pupil Book 4

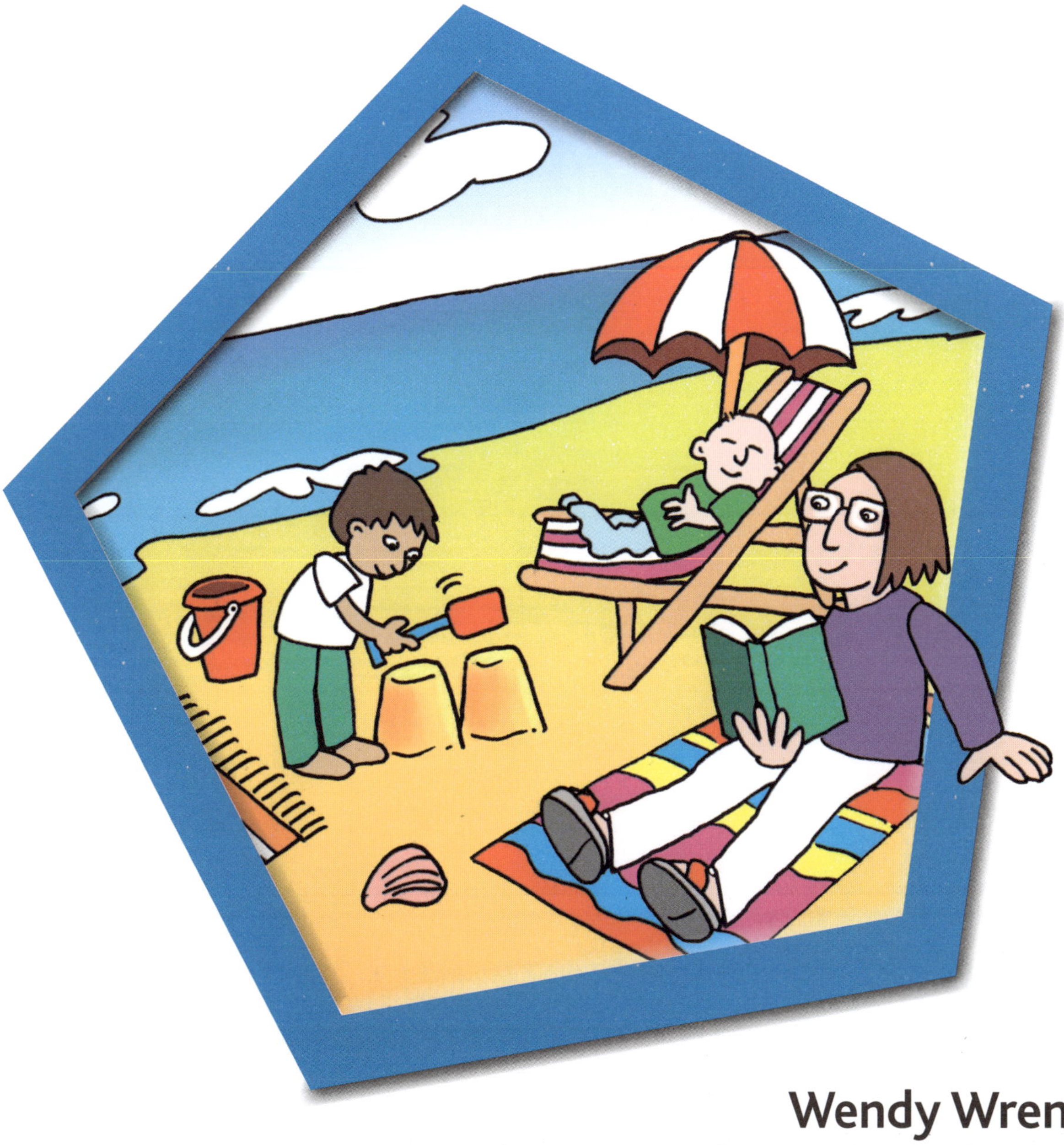

Wendy Wren
Series Editor: John Jackman

Text © Wendy Wren 2011

Original illustrations © Nelson Thornes Ltd 2011

The right of Wendy Wren to be identified as the author of this work has been asserted by them in accordance with the Copyright, Designs and Patents Act 1988.

All rights reserved. No part of this publication may be reproduced or transmitted in any form or by any means, electronic or mechanical, including photocopy, recording or any information storage and retrieval system, without permission in writing from the publisher or under licence from the Copyright Licensing Agency Limited, of Saffron House, 6–10 Kirby Street, London, EC1N 8TS.

Any person who commits any unauthorised act in relation to this publication may be liable to criminal prosecution and civil claims for damages.

Published in 2011 by:
Nelson Thornes Ltd
Delta Place
27 Bath Road
CHELTENHAM
GL53 7TH
United Kingdom

11 12 13 14 15 / 10 9 8 7 6 5 4 3 2 1

A catalogue for this book is available from the British Library

ISBN 978 1 4085 0856 5

Illustrations by Andrew Peters and Alan Rogers

Page make-up by The OKS Group

Printed by Multivista Global Ltd

Contents

Unit 1	Proper nouns	4
Unit 2	Adjectives	6
Unit 3	Confusing words	8
Unit 4	Conjunctions	10
Unit 5	Verbs	12
Unit 6	Verbs	14
Unit 7	Proper nouns	16
Check-up 1	Units 1–7	18
Unit 8	Verbs	20
Unit 9	Adjectives	22
Unit 10	Contractions	24
Unit 11	Adverbs	26
Unit 12	Prepositions	28
Unit 13	Articles	30
Check-up 2	Units 8–13	32
Unit 14	Verbs	34
Unit 15	Confusing words	36
Unit 16	Singular and plural	38
Unit 17	Adverbs	40
Unit 18	Verbs	42
Unit 19	Sentences	44
Check-up 3	Units 14–19	46

Unit 1 Proper nouns

Proper nouns are special and start with capital letters.

The names of people are proper nouns.

The names of places are proper nouns.

Sam   Kim   Midtown

                                   River Lee

Focus

A Say your answers to these questions.

1 What is the name of your friend?
2 What is the name of your teacher?
3 What is the name of the street where you live?
4 What is the name of the country you live in?

B Copy these sentences into your book. Write the **proper nouns** with capital letters.

1 A small town called greenwood is near the river mead.
2 The shops are in east street.
3 The park is in king street.
4 The town of greenwood is 40 kilometres from the sea.
5 The town is near peak mountain.

Practice

A Look at the words in the box.
Find the names of places.
Copy each **proper noun** with a capital letter.

> africa   town   egypt   india   city
> village   london   country   river
> france   new york   australia

B Use three of the proper nouns in sentences of your own.

Extension

> **TIP**
> Remember capital letters!

A Copy the sentences below.
Use a **proper noun** to fill each gap.

1 I live in _____.
2 The road I live in is called _____.
3 I would like to visit _____.
4 _____ is the name of a town.
5 _____ is the name of a country.
6 _____ is the name of a river.
7 _____ is the name of a mountain.
8 _____ is the name of my school.

B Now write your name and address.

Unit 2 Adjectives

Adjectives are describing words.
They tell us more about a person, place or thing.

TIP Colours and numbers are **adjectives**.

 **tiny** baby    **old** car

We can also use adjectives to describe the **difference between two things**.

big bottle   **bigger** bottle   **small** bike   **smaller** bike

Words like 'bigger' and 'smaller' are called **comparative adjectives**.

Focus

A Say your answers to these questions.

1. Are you **shorter** or **taller** than your friend?
2. Is the sun **bigger** or **smaller** than the Earth?

B Copy the sentences.
Add 'er' to the end of each **adjective** given in brackets.

1. My hands are (clean) than yours.
2. My radio is (loud) than yours.
3. This bread is (fresh) than those rolls.
4. It is (cold) today than it was yesterday.

Practice

A Make these adjectives into **comparative adjectives** by adding 'er'.

1. high   2. warm   3. old

B Copy the sentences below. Fill each gap with a comparative adjective that you made in **A**.

1. I can jump _____ than you.
2. I am _____ than my baby sister.
3. When the weather gets _____, I will not wear a coat.

Extension

TIP
Comparative adjectives **compare** things.

A Write these headings in your book.

Adjective	Comparative adjective

B Copy the **adjectives** in the box under the correct heading.

cold	straight	thicker	sharp
softer	smooth	colder	straighter
great	smoother	greater	soft
small	sharper	thick	smaller

C Use these **comparative adjectives** in sentences of your own.

1. weaker   2. shorter   3. hotter
4. darker   5. lower   6. tighter

Unit 3 Confusing words

TIP 'Two' written as a number is 2.

It is easy to mix up the words 'two', 'to' and 'too'.
'Two' is a number.
In **two** days it will be my birthday.
We use 'to' like this:
I am going **to** the park.
'To' is also part of a verb family name, such as:
to play   **to** fall   **to** eat
'Too' means 'as well'.
I am going to the park and Sam is coming **too**.
'Too' can also mean 'more than'.
This hill is **too** hard for me to climb.
These books are **too** heavy for me to carry.

Focus

A Talk about these questions.

1 If the weather is **too** hot, what would you do? What wouldn't you do?
2 Is it **too** far for you **to** walk **to** school?
3 If your homework is **too** hard, what would you do?

B Copy the sentences.
Fill each gap with 'two' or 'too'.

1 Please find _____ pencils for me.
2 I would like an ice lolly _____.
3 I have _____ letters to post.
4 It is _____ late to go out.
5 If we go to the park, my sister wants to come _____.

Practice

Copy the sentences.
Fill each gap with 'to' or 'too'.

1. I want .... play the piano.
2. I want to play the piano ....
3. Do you think it will be .... hard .... learn?
4. You can learn if you really want ....
5. I do want .... learn .... play.

Extension

A Copy the sentences.
Fill the gaps with 'two', 'to' or 'too'.

1. The .... times table is easy.
2. I am going .... a party today.
3. I am .... tired .... stay up late.
4. If you get .... many spellings wrong, you will have .... learn them again.
5. I have made .... mistakes.

B This sentence uses the words 'two', 'to' and 'too'.

The **two** boys ran **to** the tree but it was **too** hard **to** climb.

Now make up your own sentence using 'two', 'to' and 'too'.

Unit 4 Conjunctions

TIP: **Conjunctions** stick sentences together.

Conjunctions are words we use to join sentences.
The conjunctions 'and' and 'but' are often used to join sentences.
I put my books in my bag **and** I went to school.
I put my books in my bag **but** I forgot my pen.

Two other useful conjunctions are 'because' and 'so'.

I don't eat pizza **because** I don't like it.

Put the chairs on the table **so** I can sweep the floor.

Focus

A Which would you say?

1. I had a drink because/so I was thirsty.
2. The cat chased the mouse because/so it ran into a hole.
3. I went to bed early because/so I was tired.
4. I was hungry because/so I made a sandwich.

B Use 'because' or 'so' to join each pair of sentences. Write them in your book.

1. The lion goes hunting. It is hungry.
2. Close the hutch. The rabbit will not get out.
3. I climbed on the log. I could see over the fence.
4. Go to the shop now. It is closing soon.

Practice

TIP
'I', 'he', 'she', 'it', 'we' and 'they' are pronouns.

A Copy the sentences. Change the underlined words into **pronouns**.

1. My brother and I woke up early.
   <u>My brother and I</u> heard two birds singing.

2. The football fans cheered.
   <u>The football fans</u> saw their team score a goal.

3. Tom lost the door key.
   <u>Tom</u> could not get in.

4. Kim sat under a tree.
   <u>Kim</u> didn't get too hot.

B Join each pair of sentences you have made in  with 'because' or 'so'.

Extension

Use a **conjunction** from the box to complete each of these sentences. Write the sentences.

> and
> so
> but
> because

1. Find a cloth _____ wipe the table.
2. The door was locked _____ the window was open.
3. I don't read when I go to bed _____ I am too tired.
4. I get up early _____ I am not late for school.
5. I will eat rice _____ carrots _____ I won't eat potatoes.

11

Unit 5 Verbs

Verbs are doing or active words. Verbs that tell us what is happening now are **present tense** verbs. This is called the **simple present tense**.

The boy **kicks** the football.
He **scores** a goal.

Focus

A Which would you say?

1. I **ride** my bike. or I **rides** my bike.
2. He **eat** his apple. or He **eats** his apple.
3. They **play** football. or They **plays** football.
4. You **read** a book. or You **reads** a book.

B Copy the sentences. Underline the **simple present tense verbs**.

1. I clean my teeth.
2. I wash my face.
3. I eat my breakfast.
4. I go to school.

C Use a simple present tense verb from the box to finish each sentence.

1. The girls _____ to school.
2. The teacher _____ the homework.
3. Kim _____ her car.
4. The bird _____ in the morning.

marks
sings
drives
walk

Practice

Copy the sentences below. Change the verb family name in brackets to a **simple present tense verb**.

1. The train (to pull) into the station.
2. The people (to get) off when it stops.
3. They (to meet) their friends.
4. The train (to leave) the station.

Extension

 A Copy the table.
Fill in the missing **simple present tense verbs**.

Verb family name	Present tense
to know	I _____ he _____
to _____	we climb she _____
_____ give	it _____ they _____
to sleep	you _____ it _____

 B

1. Choose three **verb family names** from the table. Use them in sentences of your own.
2. Choose three simple present tense verbs from the table. Use them in sentences of your own.

Unit 6 Verbs

A very special **verb family** is the verb 'to be'.
Verbs can be **singular** or **plural**.
Here is the present tense of the verb 'to be'.

Singular	Plural
I am	we are
you are	you are
he/she/it is	they are

TIP
Singular means 'one'.
Plural means 'more than one'.

Focus

A Which would you say?

1. I **am** hungry.   or   I **is** hungry.
2. We **is** happy.   or   We **are** happy.
3. He **is** asleep.   or   He **are** asleep.
4. It **are** cold.   or   It **is** cold.
5. They **is** playing.   or   They **are** playing.

B Copy the sentences.
Fill each gap with the correct part of the verb 'to be'.

1. I _____ taller than my brother.
2. You _____ the youngest in the family.
3. My sister _____ playing with the cat.
4. He _____ called Jake.
5. She _____ very small.
6. They _____ my brother and sister.

Practice

Copy the sentences below.
Choose the correct word to finish each sentence.

1. The girl is/are very quiet.
2. The children is/are singing.
3. I am/is asleep by nine o'clock.
4. We am/are in the football team.
5. It is/am going to rain.
6. You is/are the best footballer in the team.

Extension

A Match the **pronouns** in the box on the left to the words in the box on the right to make sentences.

You	is the only boy.
I	are in the shop.
He	are late for school.
They	am very tired.

B Find the mistake in each sentence. Write each sentence correctly.

1. We am farmers.
2. You is a police officer.

3. He am a vet.
4. I are a doctor.

Unit 7 Proper nouns

The names of people and places are **proper nouns**.
Proper nouns have capital letters.

Mrs **G**reen   **J**ohn   **E**gypt   **R**iver **D**ee

Days of the week and months of the year are also proper nouns.
Wednesday   **S**aturday   **M**ay   **O**ctober

Focus

A Say your answers to these questions.

1 What is the month of your birthday?

2 What is a day you go to school?

3 What is a day you don't go to school?

4 What is the first day of the week?

B Copy the following **proper nouns**. Begin each one with a **capital letter**.

1 Days of the week:

__unday   __onday   __uesday
__ednesday   __hursday   __riday   __aturday

2 Months of the year:

__anuary   __ebruary   __arch   __pril
__ay   __une   __uly   __ugust
__eptember   __ctober   __ovember   __ecember

Practice

Copy the sentences. Use a day of the week or a month of the year to fill each gap.

1 .... is the first month of the year.
2 .... is the last month of the year.
3 .... comes after Monday.
4 .... and .... are called the weekend.
5 .... is the middle of the week.
6 .... is the fifth month of the year.

Extension

Special days like festivals are also **proper nouns**.

Chinese **N**ew **Y**ear   **R**amadan

Copy these sentences. Use capital letters for the proper nouns.

1 eid is a festival that marks the end of ramadan.
2 The festival of diwali is in late october or early november.
3 christmas day is on 25th december.
4 Many countries have a harvest festival.
5 The first day of january is new year's day.

Check-up 1

Proper nouns

Copy these sentences.
Write the **proper nouns** with capital letters.

1. I am going sailing on the river dee on tuesday.
2. The bus goes to midtown on saturday.
3. We are going to america in june.
4. My birthday is in february.
5. My neighbour, mrs brown, has been to china.

Adjectives

Write the missing **comparative adjectives**.

1. This torch is bright.   That torch is _____.
2. This coat is old.   That coat is _____.
3. This road is long.   That road is _____.
4. This man is strong.   That man is _____.
5. This bag is light.   That bag is _____.

Confusing words

Copy the sentences.
Choose the correct word to finish each sentence.

1. It is to/too late to go out.
2. I have got too/two minutes to/too catch the bus.
3. Can I come too/to?
4. The cat likes two/to chase the mouse.

Conjunctions

Join each pair of sentences with a **conjunction**.

1. I hurt my hand. I cannot write.
2. The girls played well. They won the match.
3. I did not feel well. I had a headache.
4. Amy was late. She missed the bus.
5. I had my sandwich. I was still hungry.

Verbs

A Copy these sentences.
Change each verb family name given in brackets to a **present tense verb**.

1. The tree (to grow) near the river.
2. People (to watch) the match.
3. The owl (to hunt) at night.
4. He (to eat) bread for breakfast.
5. She (to read) her book every day.

B Copy the sentences.
Choose the correct word to finish each sentence.

1. The boys am/are on bicycles.
2. Our cat is/am lost.
3. My brother and I is/are in the team.
4. We am/are going into town.
5. I are/am very tired.
6. You are/am older than me.

Unit 8 Verbs

The **simple present tense** of a verb tells us about something happening now.

The owl **hoots**.   The girl **runs**.

There is another present tense.
This present tense tells us about an action that is happening now and is still going on.
It is called the **present continuous tense**.

We make it like this.

verb 'to be'	+ verb	+ ing	present continuous.
I am	+ eat	+ ing	= I am eating.
You are	+ walk	+ ing	= You are walking.
He/She/It is	+ look	+ ing	= He/She/It is looking.
We are	+ talk	+ ing	= We are talking.
You are	+ stand	+ ing	= You are standing.
They are	+ cry	+ ing	= They are crying.

Focus

A Which would you say?

1. I **am** riding my bike.   or   I **is** riding my bike.
2. We **is** working hard.   or   We **are** working hard.
3. He **am** reading his book.   or   He **is** reading his book.

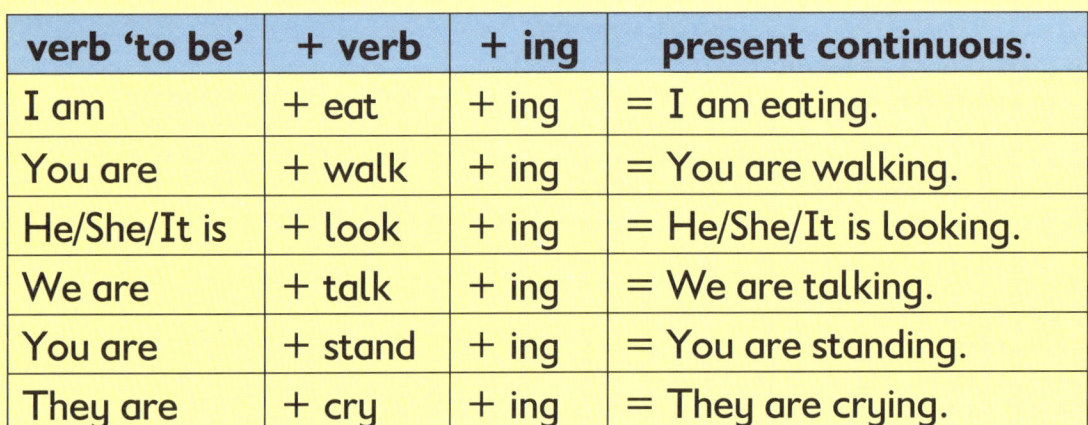

B Copy the sentences. Underline the two words in each sentence that make up the **present continuous tense**.

1. The birds are making a nest.
2. The cow is eating the grass.
3. The tree is moving in the wind.

Practice

TIP: The verb family names will help you.

Copy the sentences. Change each verb family name to a **present continuous tense verb**. Use the helper verb 'to be' and an 'ing' word.

1. Anne (to lick) her ice cream.
2. We (to play) in the park.
3. I (to read) my book.
4. It (to rain) hard.

Extension

TIP: Watch your spelling! Take off the 'e' at the end of a word before adding 'ing'.

A Copy the table. Fill in the missing parts of the **verbs**.

Verb family name	Present tense
to watch	he is _____
_____ buy	we are _____
to smile	you are _____
_____	they _____ writing
to look	it _____
_____ fall	I _____
to work	she _____

B Add 'ing' to each of these verbs.

1. talk
2. hit
3. run
4. like
5. put
6. grow
7. start
8. shine
9. park

C Add each of the words you made in **B** to the verb 'to be' to make sentences of your own.

Unit 9 Adjectives

> **TIP**
> 'Wider' is a **comparative adjective**.

We can use **adjectives** to describe the difference between two things.

 wide building   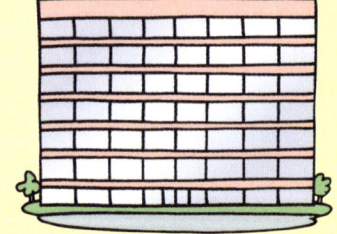 **wider** building

We can also use adjectives to describe the difference between three or more things.

 small flower    smaller flower    **smallest** flower

'Smallest' is a **superlative adjective**.
We add 'est' to an adjective when we compare three or more things.

Focus

A Say your answers to these questions.

1 What is the **longest** river in the world?
2 What is the **highest** mountain in the world?
3 What is the **biggest** ocean in the world?
4 What is the **tallest** building in the world?

B Copy these sentences. Add 'est' to each **adjective** given in brackets.

1 This building is the (tall) in town.
2 That is the (bright) star in the sky.
3 Mia is the (young) girl in her class.
4 This is the (strong) rope we sell.

Practice

Copy the sentences. Fill each gap with a **superlative adjective** from the box.

> highest   hardest   saddest
> biggest   warmest

1. An elephant is the _____ animal I have seen.
2. We climbed the _____ mountain we could find.
3. I cried because it was the _____ story I have ever read.
4. Saturday was the _____ day of the week.
5. The test was the _____ I have ever done.

Extension

A Copy the table. Fill in the missing **adjectives**.

Adjective	Comparative	Superlative
tall	_____	_____
quick	_____	_____
soft	_____	_____
smooth	_____	_____
sharp	_____	_____

B Use these **superlative adjectives** in sentences of your own.

1. plainest
2. dullest
3. largest
4. lowest
5. hardest
6. thinnest

Unit 10 Contractions

> **TIP**
> If something **contracts** it gets smaller.

Contractions are words that have been made smaller because letters have been missed out.
An **apostrophe** like this ' goes in place of the missing letter or letters.

I am looking for my gloves.
I'm looking for my gloves.

I am	=	I'm	a is missed out
you are	=	you're	a is missed out
he is	=	he's	i is missed out
she is	=	she's	i is missed out
it is	=	it's	i is missed out
we are	=	we're	a is missed out
they are	=	they're	a is missed out

Focus

A Say what the **contraction** of each word is.

1. it is
2. we are
3. she is
4. you are
5. I am
6. he is
7. they are

B The **apostrophe** has been missed out of each contraction.
Copy each contraction and put the apostrophe in the correct place.

1. we are = were
2. he is = hes
3. I am = Im
4. they are = theyre
5. you are = youre
6. she is = shes
7. it is = its

Practice

A Write the words from which these **contractions** are made.

1. she's
2. they're
3. we're
4. he's
5. it's
6. you're
7. I'm

B Copy the sentences below.
Make the underlined words into contractions.

1. I am not happy.
2. If she is late she will miss the bus.
3. They are going to meet the train.
4. It is colder than it was yesterday.
5. He is playing football after school.
6. We are on the bus.
7. When you are at the shops can you buy me a newspaper?

Extension

Can you work out which words in the box on the left match the **contractions** in the box on the right?
Write them like this: I am = I'm

> **TIP**
> Put the **apostrophe** in the space, not above a letter.

I will	I've
we are	it'll
can not	didn't
I have	she'd
she had	I'll
do not	who's
would not	don't
it will	can't
did not	wouldn't
who is	we're

Unit 11 Adverbs

TIP
Adverbs add to verbs.

An **adverb** tells us more about 'how', 'when' or 'where' an action of a verb takes place.

The boy is shouting **loudly**.
The adverb 'loudly' tells us how the boy is shouting.

Mrs Green must go **today**.
The adverb 'today' tells us when Mrs Green must go.

I have put the books **here**.
The adverb 'here' tells us where the books have been put.

Focus

A Say if the **adverb** is telling you how, when or where.

1. I am doing my homework **carefully**.
2. The boy is playing **outside**.
3. I am going to town **tomorrow**.
4. I put my shoes just **there**.
5. She sang **quietly** to the baby.

B Write a list of the adverbs used in these sentences.

1. We put the cat outside when it is dark.
2. Sam carefully coloured the picture.
3. She always buys flowers in the market.
4. It rained heavily all day.
5. I get up early on Saturdays.

Practice

A Write these headings in your book.

How	When	Where

B Read the **adverbs** in the box.

C Put each adverb under the correct heading.

> slowly   later   outside
> here   angrily   never
> sweetly   neatly   yesterday

Extension

A Finish these sentences with **adverbs**.

1 The boy sang ....
2 The boy shouted ....
3 The boy ran ....
4 The boy waved ....
5 The boy slept ....

B Use adverbs to write answers to these questions.

1 When will you do your homework?
2 How do you travel to school?
3 Where do you go shopping?
4 When can you come out to play?
5 How do you clean your teeth?
6 Where do you catch the bus?

27

Unit 12 Prepositions

Prepositions tell us where something is.

The cat is **on** the roof.

B comes **after** A in the alphabet.

Focus

A Make up a sentence using each of these **prepositions**.

1. on 2. up 3. behind 4. outside

B Copy the sentences below.
Choose the correct **preposition** from the box to fill each gap.

> through
> behind
> between
> in

1. The water is _____ the pan.

2. The house is in _____ the trees.

3. The snake is _____ the rock.

4. The path goes _____ the wood.

28

Practice

Look carefully at the picture. Write some sentences about the picture. Use a **preposition** in each sentence.

Extension

A Copy the sentences. Choose the correct **preposition** to fill each gap.

1 I am very angry for / with you.
2 The medicine is good for / of you
3 I know I can rely in / on you.
4 Put the letter in / on the postbox.

B Use these prepositions in sentences of your own.

1 without   2 after   3 before   4 under
5 around   6 inside   7 at   8 beneath

Unit 13 Articles

The words 'a' and 'an' are called **articles**.

We use 'a' before words starting with a **consonant**.

We use 'an' before words starting with a **vowel**.

a jungle

an orange

TIP
The **vowels** are: 'a', 'e', 'i', 'o', 'u'. The other letters are **consonants**.

Focus

A Say if you would use 'a' or 'an'.

1. _____ girl
2. _____ owl
3. _____ village
4. _____ umbrella
5. _____ ship
6. _____ piano

B In your book, write 'a' or 'an' in front of each of these words.

1. _____ elephant
2. _____ car
3. _____ toffee

4. _____ apple
5. _____ insect
6. _____ carrot

Practice

A Write the ten words from this box that you would use with 'an'.

> oak cap sun eel rug rat egg table card ear
> inch box owl ant log oar arm fox ark mat

B Copy these sentences. Write 'a' or 'an' in the gaps.

1. _____ owl sat in _____ tree.
2. I put _____ book, _____ pencil and _____ apple in my bag.
3. We had _____ idea.
4. I have _____ exam next week.
5. I have _____ uncle and _____ aunt.

Extension

We use 'an' before a silent 'h'.
It is **an h**onour to be made team captain.

We use 'a' before 'u' and 'eu' when the sound is 'y' as in 'yes'.
A metre is **a** unit of length.

A Write 'a' or 'an' before these words.

1. _____ uniform
2. _____ house
3. _____ hour
4. _____ umbrella
5. _____ udder
6. _____ hotel

Check-up 2

Verbs

Write the **verb** in each sentence.

1. I write very neatly.
2. The bird is pecking at the ground.
3. He works hard at school.
4. They are waiting for the train.

Adjectives

A Write the **comparatives** of these adjectives.

1. sick   2. short   3. smooth

B Write the **superlatives** of these adjectives.

1. sad   2. smart   3. flat

C Use these adjectives to write sentences of your own.

1. happy   2. louder   3. easiest

Contractions

Write the **contractions** for these words.

1. she is   2. we are   3. it is   4. they are
5. I am   6. he is   7. you are

Adverbs

A Sort these **adverbs** into how, when and where adverbs.

> before   unhappily   often   far   nowhere
> high   untidily   soon   quickly

B Make these sentences more interesting by adding adverbs.

1. The sun shone _____.
2. The bird flew _____.
3. They ran _____ in the race.
4. They swam _____ in the river.

Prepositions

A Write all the **prepositions** you can find in this story.

The fox ran behind the dustbin and leaped on the fence. It jumped into a tree and ran along a branch. The fox got down from the tree and went through a hedge. It looked around, went inside a shed and hid between some old boxes.

B Use these prepositions to write sentences of your own.

1. over   2. between   3. among   4. after

Articles

Write 'a' or 'an' in front of each word.

1. arm   2. city   3. umbrella   4. bag
5. house   6. uniform   7. ant   8. bicycle
9. orange   10. shop   11. hour   12. oven

Unit 14 Verbs

Verbs are 'doing' or 'active' words.

We use **present tense verbs** for what is happening now.

We use **past tense verbs** for something that happened in the past.

The frog **jumps** into the pond.
The frog **is jumping** into the pond.

The frog **jumped** into the pond.

To make the past tense we usually add 'ed' to the verb family name.

If the verb family name ends in 'e', we just add 'd'.

to talk   **talked**   to wave   **waved**

Focus

A Say what the **past tense** of each verb is.

1. to look
2. to walk
3. to bake
4. to wash
5. to shout
6. to listen
7. to glue
8. to paint

B Copy the sentences. Underline the **past tense verb**.

1. We wanted to go out.
2. We voted to go ice skating.
3. We played all afternoon.
4. I needed a rest later.
5. I enjoyed the book.
6. I stroked the cat.

Practice

TIP
Find the **verb**. Think of its family name then add 'ed' or 'd'.

Copy the sentences below. Change the **present tense verbs** into the **past tense**.

1. The children cook pizza for tea.
2. I look for a good book to read.
3. The boys laugh at the joke.

Extension

A Copy this table. Fill in the missing words.

Verb family name	Present tenses	Past tense
to chew	she _____ he is _____	they chewed
to watch	we watch they _____	I _____
to _____	I paint he _____ painting	we _____
to finish	you _____ you _____	it _____
to _____	they ask I _____	he _____

B Use these **past tense verbs** in sentences of your own.

1. whispered
2. stopped
3. picked
4. called
5. posted
6. cleaned

Unit 15 Confusing words

TIP
Look for the word 'here' in 'where' and 'there'. 'Here' also means a place.

We sometimes confuse words because they sound similar.
We can mix up the words 'where', 'were' and 'we're'.

'Where' usually means a place.	**Where** are you going?
We use 'were' when we are talking about something that happened in the past.	They **were** off school the day before yesterday.
'We're' is a contraction for 'we are'.	**We're** doing our homework.

We can also mix up these three words: 'there', 'their' and 'they're'.

'There' usually means a place.	The park is over **there**.
'Their' means 'belonging to them'.	They got **their** coats dirty.
'They're' is a contraction for 'they are'.	**They're** not here.

Focus

A Which would you say?

1. **Where** is the book?   or   **We're** is the book?
2. **Were** late.   or   **We're** late.
3. They **where** cooking.   or   They **were** cooking.
4. Put it over **there**.   or   Put it over **they're**.
5. They got **there** books.   or   They got **their** books.
6. **Their** sleeping.   or   **They're** sleeping.

B Copy these sentences.
Choose the correct word to fill each gap.

1 Where/Were are you going?
2 If were/we're late we won't get in.
3 I think we catch the bus over there/their.
4 Where/We're did you find they're/their hats?

Practice

A Copy the sentences below.
Choose 'where', 'were' or 'we're' to fill each gap.

1 Many people _____ going to see the match.
2 "_____ almost there," said Dad.
3 "_____ do we go when we get inside?" I asked.

B Copy these sentences.
Choose 'there', 'their' or 'they're' to fill each gap

1 Tom and Kim played with _____ cat.
2 _____ playing with a ball.

Extension

TIP
Look back at Unit 3 to remind you about 'two', 'to' and 'too'.

A Choose the correct word to fill each gap.

1 There/Their is nothing left to/two eat.
2 Tell me we're/where I can go too/to buy some food.
3 The best place to/two go is over there/they're.

B Use these words in sentences of your own.

1 where   2 two   3 they're   4 were
5 too   6 their   7 we're   8 there

Unit 16 Singular and plural

Singular means one person or thing. **Plural** means 'more than one' person or thing.

We usually add 's' to a noun to make it plural.

Some nouns need 'es' on the end to make them plural. These nouns end in:

one eagle   two eagles

Ending	Singular	Plural
ch	mat**ch**	match**es**
sh	wi**sh**	wish**es**
s	bu**s**	bus**es**
ss	gla**ss**	glass**es**
x	bo**x**	box**es**

Focus

A Read the words.
Do they need 's' or 'es' to make them **plural**?

1. town
2. patch
3. farmer
4. box
5. stitch
6. guess
7. rash
8. doctor

B Make these singular nouns plural.
Write them in your book.

1. dish
2. trench
3. punch
4. grass
5. fox
6. cross
7. ditch
8. rash
9. gas
10. march
11. gash
12. finch

C Use five of your **plural nouns** from **B** in sentences of your own.

Practice

Copy this table.
Fill in the missing **singular** and **plural** nouns.

Singular	Plural	Singular	Plural
bush	----------	----------	compasses
arch	----------	splash	----------
----------	gashes	table	----------
tax	----------	crash	----------
tree	----------	torch	----------

Extension

 Write the **plural nouns** ending in 'es' that match these descriptions. The pictures will help you.

1

We use these to tell the time.

w _ _ _ _ e s

2

These books have maps of countries in them.

a _ _ _ _ e s

3

Girls sometimes wear these.

d _ _ _ _ e s

4

These are the daughters of a king and queen.

p _ _ _ _ _ _ _ e s

 Use three of the plural nouns you have made in in sentences of your own.

Unit 17 Adverbs

An **adverb** tells us more about how, when or where the action of a verb takes place.

How	The lightning flashed **brightly**.
When	The thunder rumbled **later**.
Where	The rain fell **here**.

Adverbs are sometimes used in pairs to make the meaning clearer.

I walked **more slowly** than my friend.

These adverbs can also tell us more about other adverbs:

quite   only   so   almost   very   rather   less   most

Focus

A Say your answers to these questions.

1. If you do your work **less quickly** than your friend, who finishes first?
2. If you swim **very often**, do you swim a lot or not?
3. If you listen to your teachers **most carefully**, are you paying attention or not?

B Write in your book the **pair of adverbs** from each sentence.

1. The cat moved rather slowly towards the bird.
2. The bird hopped about quite happily.
3. Very quietly, the cat moved closer.
4. Almost silently, the cat jumped towards the bird.
5. The bird flew very quickly into a tree.

Practice

A Choose a different **adverb** from the box to improve the meaning of each sentence.

> more   very   so   rather   less   extremely

1. Put away the glasses _____ carefully.
2. You need to paint _____ colourfully.
3. When we move away, we will visit _____ often.
4. The train is running _____ late.

B Use these **pairs of adverbs** in sentences of your own.

1. rather slowly
2. very quickly
3. more quietly

Extension

Improve this story by adding at least six **adverbs** or **pairs of adverbs**.

Night fell and the wood was dark and gloomy. The two friends rode on their horses and talked. They heard a noise in the trees and stopped. One of the men got off his horse and listened. They heard the noise again.

"What shall we do?" whispered the man on the horse.

"I don't know," the other man said.

"I think we should ride on and get out of this wood."

The man got back on his horse and the two friends left the wood.

Unit 18 Verbs

To put a **verb** in the **simple past tense**, we usually add 'd' or 'ed' to the verb family name.

Verb family	Past tense
to argue	argue**d**
to look	look**ed**

Some verbs do not follow this rule.
The verb 'to be' is one of them. Here it's the **past tense**. It is useful to learn this.

Singular	Plural
I was	we were
you were	you were
he/she/it was	they were

Sometimes we need to change the middle vowel sound to make the simple past tense.

Present tense   sing   write
Past tense   sang   wrote

Focus

 **A** Say what the **simple past tense** of each verb is.

1. to move
2. to paint
3. to walk
4. to laugh
5. to smile
6. to follow

 B Match the **simple present tense verbs** in the box on the left with the **simple past tense verbs** in the box on the right. Write the pairs in your book.

| grow make come jump | held grew played came |
| hold draw play shine | drew shone jumped made |

Practice

Copy the sentences below.
Change the verb in brackets to the **simple past tense**.

1. We (arrive) at school early.
2. I (mix) the paints.
3. I (paint) a picture of my house.
4. We (play) a spelling game.
5. My team (come) first.
6. I (am) very pleased.

Extension

Some verbs do not follow any rules to help you make the **simple past tense**.

For example, the simple past tense of the verb 'to go' is 'went'.

A Write the simple past tense of these verbs. Use a dictionary to help you.

1. to go
2. to leave
3. to speak
4. to catch
5. to find
6. to have
7. to meet
8. to eat
9. to sleep
10. to say
11. to write
12. to think

B Copy the sentences below. Choose the correct **verb** to fill each gap so the sentences are in the simple past tense.

1. I am/was cross with my friend.
2. The day was/is cold and damp.
3. The children ran/run across the field.
4. The rain fall/fell all day.
5. The sun shine/shone the next day.

Unit 19 Sentences

Every sentence must make sense.
There are three things every sentence needs to help it make sense.

a capital letter   **a full stop**

The eagle **flew** over the mountain**.**

a verb

Focus

A Say what the **verb** in each sentence is.

1. I want a new pencil.
2. We are going on the bus.
3. We found an old football.
4. He is very tired.
5. The girl has a book.
6. She taught us some new words.

B Copy these sentences. Give each sentence a capital letter and a full stop. Underline the verb.

1. the wind blew around the house
2. my family lives in the country
3. i am sitting in my chair
4. we are going on holiday
5. the stone cracked the window
6. the boy fell on the steps
7. the gate creaked in the wind
8. they are playing in the park

TIP
Be careful! Some of the sentences have two verbs working together.

Practice

Choose a **verb** from the box to make each of these into a sensible sentence.

> is   bought   is painting
> am looking   used

1. He _____ a picture.
2. This flower _____ very beautiful.
3. We _____ our new pens today.
4. I _____ for my reading book.
5. Mum _____ fruit at the market.

Extension

A Add a **simple past tense verb** to complete each sentence.

1. Sam _____ into the house.
2. The thunder _____ him.
3. The rain _____ quickly.
4. The lightning _____ across the sky.
5. He _____ under the bedclothes.

B Use each of these **verbs** in sentences of your own. Remember the capital letters and full stops.

1. am flying
2. is looking
3. closed
4. are making
5. dug
6. swam
7. am building
8. played

Check-up 3

Proper nouns

Copy these sentences.
Write the **proper nouns** with a capital letter.

1 The river thames runs through london.
2 new year's day is hot in australia.
3 cairo is the capital of egypt.

Adjectives

A Read and copy the description.
Fill in the gaps with interesting **adjectives**.

The _____ house is by the side of a _____ road. There is a _____ garden at the front and the back. There is a _____ garage next to the house. _____ trees grow around the house, making it _____ and _____.

B Make the adjectives in brackets into **comparative adjectives**.

1 That piece of cake is (small) than this one.
2 There is a (long) piece of string on the table.
3 The river is (deep) by the other bank.
4 The blue car is (fast) than the red car.

C Make the adjectives in brackets into **superlative adjectives**.

1 This is the (high) of all the hills.
2 Use the (clean) cloth you can find.
3 This is the (sad) story I have read.

Confusing words

Choose the correct words to complete the story.

In too / two days' time, were / we're going to / too visit our cousins. Their / There house is in the country and where / we're going by train. Were / Where they live is very beautiful because their / there is a river and a lake two / too.

Contractions

Write the **contractions** of these pairs of words.

1 he is
2 I am
3 they are
4 it is
5 did not
6 who is
7 would not
8 we are

Verbs

A Write the **past tense** of these verbs.

1 to walk
2 to give
3 to buy
4 to go
5 to think
6 to play
7 to find
8 to write

B Change these sentences from the present tense to the **past tense**.

1 We swim in the sea.
2 I run for the bus.

C Change these sentences from the past tense to the **present tense**.

1. Many people played football.
2. The children sang every morning.
3. The elephants liked water.
4. The sun was shining.

D Choose the correct word for each sentence.

1. The plants is/are growing well.
2. I am/is writing a letter.
3. We was/were told to go outside.

Adverbs

Copy the sentences. Add **adverbs** to fill the gaps.

1. I went to the shops ⎯⎯⎯⎯.
2. He did his work ⎯⎯⎯⎯.
3. The boy laughed ⎯⎯⎯⎯.
4. I tidied my room ⎯⎯⎯⎯.

Prepositions

Use these **prepositions** in sentences of your own.

1. between
2. over
3. through
4. in
5. under
6. near

Articles

Write 'a' or 'an' in front of each word.

1. bush
2. ant
3. hour
4. hero
5. umbrella
6. island
7. donkey
8. uniform